FANTASTIC BEASTS
AND WHERE TO FIND THEM™

THE BEASTS

CINEMATIC GUIDE

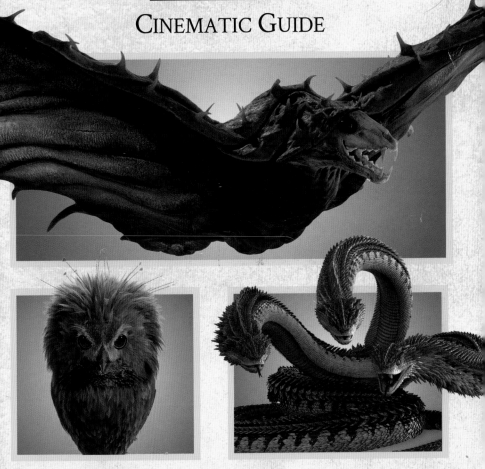

J.K. ROWLING'S · WIZARDING WORLD

SCHOLASTIC LTD.

www.fantasticbeasts.co.uk

Scholastic Children's Books
Euston House, 24 Eversholt Street,
London NW1 1DB, UK

A division of Scholastic Ltd
London ~ New York ~ Toronto ~ Sydney ~ Auckland
Mexico City ~ New Delhi ~ Hong Kong

First published in the US by Scholastic Inc, 2017
Published in the UK by Scholastic Ltd, 2017

By Felicity Baker
Art Direction: Rick DeMonico
Page Design: Heather Barber

ISBN 978 1407 17339 9

Printed in the UK by Bell and Bain Ltd, Glasgow

2 4 6 8 10 9 7 5 3 1

www.scholastic.co.uk

CONTENTS

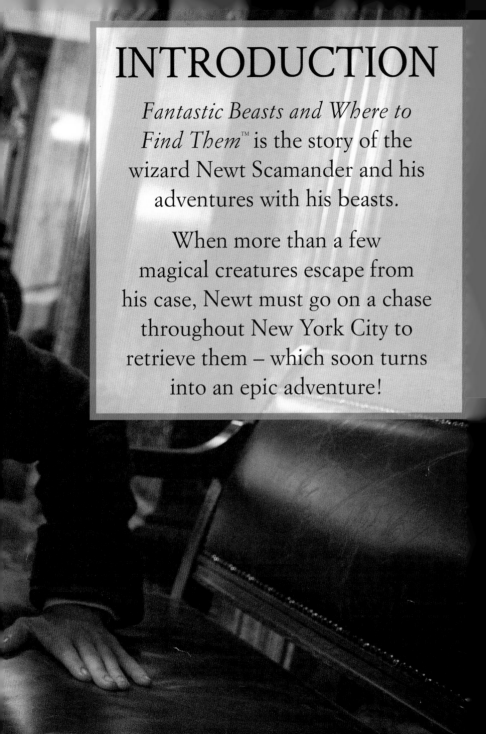

INTRODUCTION

Fantastic Beasts and Where to Find Them™ is the story of the wizard Newt Scamander and his adventures with his beasts.

When more than a few magical creatures escape from his case, Newt must go on a chase throughout New York City to retrieve them – which soon turns into an epic adventure!

Magizoology is the study of magical creatures – the fantastic beasts who are part of the wizarding world, outside of No-Maj awareness.

Currently, there is only one known Magizoologist: Newt Scamander. Newt feels more comfortable around beasts than he does around humans.

Newt is working on a manuscript entitled *Fantastic Beasts and Where to Find Them* to educate the wizarding community about the beauty and importance of magical creatures.

Newton ("Newt") Artemis Fido Scamander
has a mission: to find and study all the fantastic
beasts in existence, either in their natural
habitats or in ones he recreates in his case.

Newt attended Hogwarts School of Witchcraft and Wizardry where
he was sorted into Hufflepuff house. While a student at Hogwarts,
Newt was caught up in an unfortunate incident in which he took
the blame for another student's life-endangering mistake. Despite
Professor Dumbledore's pleas, Newt was still expelled.

"WHAT MAKES ALBUS DUMBLEDORE SO FOND OF YOU, MR SCAMANDER?"

-PERCIVAL GRAVES

When the Great War raged, Newt worked with the Ministry of Magic on a classified programme to wrangle dragons. He commanded Ukrainian Ironbellies, but the Ministry cancelled the programme because the unruly dragons tried to devour everyone *but* Newt. After the war ended, Newt ventured across the globe to write a book on Magizoology that would serve as both a record of his observations and as a learning tool for others.

NEWT'S CASE

To protect the beasts he finds, some of which are endangered, Newt provides habitats called biomes for them inside his leather case – however unbelievable that may seem!

On the outside, Newt's brown case looks like it could be purchased at any leather goods shop. In fact, Newt's adventure in New York City begins *because* of how ordinary his case looks.

While at Steen National Bank, Newt meets Jacob Kowalski, a person without any magical abilities, which in America is called a No-Maj. Jacob accidentally takes Newt's case thinking it is his own!

The thing that sets Newt's case apart is that it has two different modes, activated by switching a special lock. In the first mode, "Muggle Worthy", the case opens to reveal various personal effects. In the second mode, the brass dial on the lock can be rotated to "Open". This transforms Newt's case into a pathway to a wholly magical environment where he keeps and cares for dozens of fantastic beasts.

Inside the world of the case, each creature lives in its own special habitat.

The beasts are comfortable inside the case, free from the worry of starvation or extermination. Nonetheless, when Newt's magical lock becomes momentarily faulty, the Niffler, an especially curious beast, slips out.

"DON'T PANIC. THERE'S ABSOLUTELY NOTHING TO WORRY ABOUT."

-NEWT SCAMANDER

When Jacob later gets home and opens up Newt's case, he unwittingly releases many of the remaining beasts, exposing New York City to chaos. Jacob even gets a nasty bite on his neck from an escaping Murtlap.

In addition to containing the beasts' habitats, the case is also home to Newt's private shed.

The shed stores everything necessary to maintain the health and well-being of Newt's beasts.

Newt also keeps equipment in his shed that he might need during his outings to catch magical creatures. There is also a typewriter on which Newt types the pages of his book.

Newt has stockpiled crates of food pellets and carefully arranged bottles such as Shell Shiner, Beak Balm, Feather Floss, Hoof Healer Ointment and more.

Newt also keeps charts about each beast's feeding and habitat needs.

Part of the shed's interior has been turned into a laboratory. Beakers and jars containing herbs and other ingredients can be found on Newt's desk and shelves.

Newt uses these ingredients to concoct his magical potions and mixes the salves that help him care for his beasts.

THE BEASTS

From charming little beasts that can fit into Newt's pocket to terrifying giants that can blast holes into brick walls, Newt's case is a safe haven for all beasts. Whether they are cuddly or inspire fear, Newt loves and cares for them all equally.

BILL

BILLYWIG

A Billywig can zip through the air so quickly
that Newt needs to zap one with his wand to
catch it. The outside of its body is a brilliant
blue, the colour of sapphires.

This Billywig soars into the sky just above a crowd of New Yorkers.
The No-Majs are oblivious, but not Tina Goldstein, a witch.

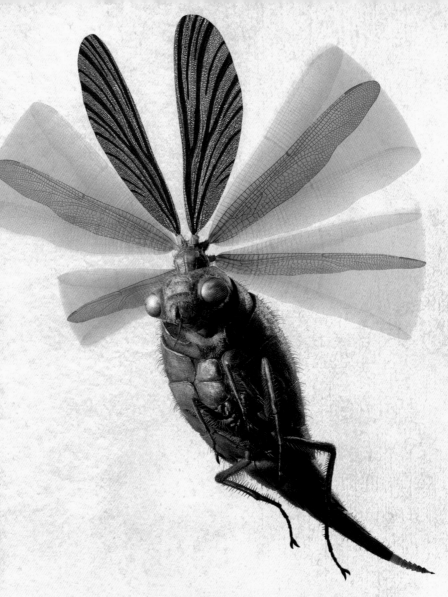

"WE'RE GOING TO RECAPTURE MY CREATURES BEFORE THEY GET HURT. THEY ARE CURRENTLY IN ALIEN TERRAIN, SURROUNDED BY MILLIONS OF THE MOST VICIOUS CREATURES ON THE PLANET. HUMANS."

–NEWT SCAMANDER

BOWTRUCKLE

Many species in the animal kingdom mimic other species. Few do it as well as the Bowtruckle. This tiny, thin creature camouflages itself into the trees it inhabits. Green roots splay from a stemlike body for legs and feet, while woody arms and fingers curve out like miniature branches on a tree. Each Bowtruckle looks different from its fellows, with different arrangements of leaves and branches.

Newt planted a small bamboo forest for the Bowtruckle community he saved and whenever he visits, these little chatterboxes rush out to welcome him.

"TITUS. FINN. JEREMY. ALL PRESENT."

—NEWT SCAMANDER TO THE BOWTRUCKLES

"PICKETT, LET GO..."

-NEWT SCAMANDER

Unlike the other Bowtruckles, Pickett prefers to reside in Newt's greatcoat rather than the bamboo forest. Recently, Pickett had an excuse to do so – he had been ill with a cold and needed Newt's body heat to get well. Now Pickett has grown attached to the warm and friendly Newt, and does not want to go back into the case. Pickett's brothers are jealous and accuse Newt of favouritism, but despite Newt's pleas, Pickett clings to him.

The anxious little Bowtruckle proves himself very helpful when Newt finds himself imprisoned by wizarding authorities inside MACUSA, the Magical Congress of the United States of America.

Pickett comes to the rescue when he inserts his twig-like limbs into the keyhole of Newt's handcuffs, successfully picking the lock and helping Newt escape MACUSA executioners.

DEMIGUISE

To spot a Demiguise in the flesh is to see one of the rarest magical creatures. It is a gangly, apelike beast who is mostly peaceful, but can give a nasty nip if provoked, as the scar on Newt's thumb shows. Its long, silver-white hair and doleful brown eyes gives it the appearance of an old, wise sage. This resemblance fits its abilities, for the Demiguise has an incredible power of precognition – an uncanny foresight of predicting the most likely events that will occur in the immediate future. This means that a Demiguise could dodge a pursuer before that pursuer has even given chase!

Trying to catch a Demiguise seems even more futile since it can become invisible. Given these talents, it's a wonder that anyone ever spotted a Demiguise in the first place.

"DEMIGUISE ARE FUNDAMENTALLY PEACEFUL, BUT THEY CAN GIVE A NASTY NIP IF PROVOKED."

—NEWT SCAMANDER

One of Newt's greatest feats could be catching Dougal, a Demiguise, when he escapes from his leather case and turns up in a department store.

To catch a beast who thrives on knowing the presumable outcome of many different future scenarios, Newt has to do the unexpected – act *unpredictably*.

"NO, NO, NO – DOUGAL'S GOT OUT! HIS ARM HAD ONLY JUST HEALED AS WELL!"

–NEWT SCAMANDER

Dougal is a mischievous creature with a sweet tooth, stealing sweets when the opportunity arises. Of course, this is not a difficult task for an invisible beast!

Dougal has a softer side as well. He tenderly babysat Newt's young Occamy from the time it was just an egg.

DOXY

The Doxy resembles a chameleon, with bulbous compound eyes that can see in multiple directions at once and the scaly skin of a lizard that changes colours to fit mood or environment. Long, multicoloured ears fan out from its head, giving it exceptional hearing ability.

Not wanting to admit that his fantastic beasts are on the loose all over New York City, Newt dismisses the Doxy that flies past as nothing more than a moth. But Newt's companion, Tina Goldstein, is a former Auror with MACUSA and is not so easily fooled.

**"IT DIDN'T LOOK
LIKE A MOTH..."**
–TINA GOLDSTEIN

ERUMPENT

The massive Erumpent can be a temperamental beast. Most of the time, it has a placid, calm nature. It eats several times its own weight in grasses on the plains – resulting in dung that can be the size of boulders! When a female Erumpent is in heat, her mating instincts can transform her into a dangerous aggressor. In such a state, she is virtually impossible to stop.

The Erumpent's dark, blubbery hide protects it from most attacks, while the horn that protrudes from its armoured head can be used as a deadly weapon. When its head changes colour, the Erumpent is ready for action.

"WHERE DO YOU THINK A... MEDIUM-
SIZED CREATURE THAT LIKES BROAD,
OPEN PLAINS — WATERHOLES,
TREES — WOULD GO?"

-NEWT SCAMANDER

One of the largest beasts that escapes from the case is a female Erumpent. In heat and searching for a mate, the Erumpent rams through an apartment wall and out into the New York City streets.

Newt and Jacob track down the Erumpent to the Central Park Zoo where she has trampled fences and cages, releasing many of the animals. Newt gives Jacob special protective clothing as a precaution.

In an effort to catch her attention, Newt dabs a bit of Erumpent musk onto his wrists. Jacob accidentally douses himself in the scent.

The beast gets one whiff of Jacob and charges right at him, her horn brightly glowing. Jacob scrambles up a nearby tree while Newt distracts the Erumpent so that she slides across a sheet of ice – right back into his open case!

FWOOPER

Though small, this birdlike beast can consume giant hunks of meat in one bite. One can only imagine that this heightened ability to swallow may have evolved from necessity due to the competition of larger animals, like the Graphorns.

GRAPHORN

The Graphorn is resistant to domestication, but Newt has successfully won the favour of the last breeding pair in existence. In fact, it's not uncommon for one to place its hooves on the Magizoologist's shoulders and lick his face or hands with its purple tongue. If Newt hadn't saved them, the species would have likely become extinct. But don't be fooled – these same beasts can also savagely rip open a carcass and feast on the meat.

MOONCALF

The Mooncalf is a darling creature with soft skin, enormous eyes and webbed feet. Newt cares for his calves in a special meadow he has magically created: the meadow always gives the appearance of a starry night with the shine of the full moon. Shy at first encounter, Mooncalves will warm up to visitors if they have treats.

At Newt's suggestion, Jacob feeds the beasts special pellets. They sidle up to him, eat from his hand and take away all of Jacob's worries and fears about the unfamiliar magical world.

"WOULD YOU MIND THROWING SOME PELLETS IN WITH THE MOONCALVES? OVER THERE, THE DARK FIELD."

-NEWT SCAMANDER TO JACOB KOWALSKI

MURTLAP

To city dwellers, the
Murtlap might look like an
oversized rat. A mass of tentacles
grows along its back, as if it had
been crossed with a sea anemone.

The Murtlap is most renowned
for its bite. For those of wizarding
blood, the bite can be beneficial,
as it provides momentary
resistance to jinxes and curses.
For No-Majs, however, the bite
usually results in an itchy rash.

Ferocity can sometimes come in small packages – which Jacob Kowalski learns in a sudden and scary confrontation with a Murtlap!

Some No-Majs are more susceptible to a Murtlap's bite, as is the case with Jacob Kowalski. In these worst cases, the reaction to the bite can be very severe: flames can erupt from the victim's rear end and a two-day period of uncomfortable itching and twitching can result.

Luckily for Jacob, Newt has a remedy and takes Jacob inside his magical case to get it. Newt gives Jacob tree sap to alleviate the constant itch and pills to calm his nervous system.

NIFFLER

The beast who proves most troublesome for
Newt during his trip to New York is the small,
harmless-looking Niffler. Though it's scarcely
larger than a mole, its hunger for shiny things
is insatiable. It has beady eyes, dark fur and a
duck-like, flesh-coloured bill like a platypus.
Oddly, its nose, rather than its eyes, leads the
Niffler on its quests. It can sniff out objects that
shine and track their luminous scent.

The pouch on its belly is where the Niffler stores
its bounty. But the Niffler isn't much of a judge
when it comes to appraising an object's worth.
As long as it shines – whether it be keys, coins or
even tooth fillings – the Niffler wants it.

"NIFFLER'S GONE, THE LITTLE PEST. ANY CHANCE TO GET HIMSELF MORE SHINY STUFF."

-NEWT SCAMANDER

Once the Niffler is out of Newt's case, it squeaks with pleasure as it picks up loose change on the street, digs through purses and tries to remove gold buckles from shoes.

The Niffler greedily breaks into the vault at Steen National Bank.

Newt and Jacob chase the Niffler to New York City's Diamond District, where it breaks into a jewellery shop. Needless to say, Newt is not pleased with the little pilfering pest – especially when the police think Newt and Jacob are the jewel thieves!

"CALM DOWN, LITTLE ONE. MUMMY'S HERE."
-NEWT SCAMANDER TO AN OCCAMY HATCHLING

OCCAMY

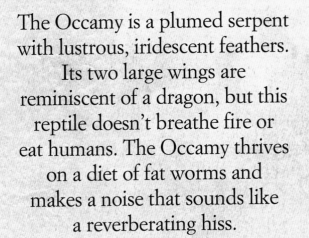

The Occamy is a plumed serpent with lustrous, iridescent feathers. Its two large wings are reminiscent of a dragon, but this reptile doesn't breathe fire or eat humans. The Occamy thrives on a diet of fat worms and makes a noise that sounds like a reverberating hiss.

One innate talent has probably kept it from extinction up to this point – the Occamy is choranaptyxic. It has the power to change its size to accommodate a given space. It can enlarge its body to fill a vast chamber or shrink down to fit into a tiny space.

"HEY, MISTER ENGLISH GUY, I THINK YOUR EGG IS HATCHING!"

-JACOB KOWALSKI

An Occamy's silver eggs fetch a pretty penny on the black market. They are so sought after that there are only a few Occamies left in existence. The creatures have learned to become quite defensive as a result.

The Occamy and its babysitter, Dougal, hide out in a local department store.

Newt devises a plan that plays on the Occamy's choranaptyxic talent and taste for insects. He instructs Tina to capture the beast inside a teapot that contains a cockroach.

It is no easy feat to catch the Demiguise and the Occamy, and the department store is left in a shambles.

RUNESPOOR

Bands of bright orange cover the body of the Runespoor and ward off predators who instinctively recognize that a colourful snake is often a venomous one. But it's not necessarily the colourful pattern that induces dread in the Runespoor's victims – it's that this serpent has three heads!

Along with those three heads come three minds of their own. The heads often bicker in disagreement and start fighting with each other, making one of the Runespoor's greatest predators *itself*.

The sight of this ferocious beast is terrifying to Jacob, who is petrified of snakes. Despite Newt's mastery of the beast, Jacob maintains a safe distance in the Runespoor's presence.

"THE LOCALS CALL IT SWOOPING EVIL — NOT THE FRIENDLIEST NAME. THEY THINK IT SUCKS OUT BRAINS — BUT IT'S QUITE USEFUL IF YOU'RE IN A FIX."

—NEWT SCAMANDER

SWOOPING EVIL

The Swooping Evil exhibits not only the
appearance but also the behaviours of both
reptiles and insects. Its reptilian body is spiked
and scaly and its mouth has fierce fangs. These
features are coupled with wings that possess the
vibrant blue coloration of a moth or butterfly.
During periods of dormancy, the Swooping Evil
transforms into a spiny cocoon. Newt finds it
useful to keep one of these in his pocket.

The Swooping Evil cocoon comes in handy when Newt and Tina are
in danger in MACUSA.

Newt tosses the cocoon into the air and the winged beast emerges, giving Newt and Tina a life-saving getaway ride.

Newt believes the Swooping Evil's venom can be useful and collects it in a vial for later experimentation. If he can properly dilute it, he thinks the venom could be used to eliminate unwanted memories.

**"THAT IS WHY I CAME TO AMERICA.
TO BRING FRANK HOME."**

—NEWT SCAMANDER

THUNDERBIRD

The eagle-like Thunderbird has six wings
and can arrange its feathers in such a way as to
present dazzling pictures of the sun and sky. At
the hint of danger, however, those feathers darken
and lightning illuminates the bird's eyes.
With just a few flaps, the Thunderbird's wings
summon a torrential storm.

The Thunderbird lives in desolate places, like
the deserts of Arizona. The beast carries a price
on its head and is often sought by hunters.

Newt rescued a Thunderbird he calls Frank from a group of poachers. Thanks to Newt, the beast has a second chance at life and the opportunity to heal.

"I WASN'T GOING TO LEAVE HIM CHAINED."

–NEWT SCAMANDER ON FRANK THE THUNDERBIRD

"I TRY TO LIVE LIKE A BEAST...
THEY DON'T FEAR THE END.
THEY CONCENTRATE ON LIVING."

–NEWT SCAMANDER